ABSORB THE COLORS

poems by
Northfield Women Poets

foreword
by MERIDEL LE SUEUR

editors

Beverly Voldseth
Karen Herseth Wee

ACKNOWLEDGMENTS

"Dinosaur Spring" first appeared in *Crazy Horse*. "Light Under the Door" first appeared in *The Ohio Review*. "Love Poem for the Nuclear Age: After the Bomb" first appeared in *Iowa Woman*, "Mama's Murders" first appeared in *The Georgia Review*.

Some of the other poems in this book previously have appeared in the *Carleton Miscellany, gathering Post, The Inkling, Loonfeather, Milkweed Chronicle, Rag Mag*, and *Sing Heavenly Muse*.

This book of poetry is made possible in part by a grant provided by the Southeastern Minnesota Arts Council Incorporated through funding from the Minnesota State Arts Board and Minnesota legislature.

Book Cover Design:
    poets' collaboration
Artwork: Riki Kölbl Nelson
Typeface: Souvenir
Printed in Northfield, Minn.
Heywood Press
Copyright 1984
ISBN 0-9614314-0-7

FOREWORD

If I am delighted with this anthology of women poets, it is because I lived in a time when this book could not have been written, published, or read. I lived in a time when women were mute, silent, invisible. Even twenty years ago this book would not have been visible. These poems, if written at all, would have been written in secrecy and in danger of being destroyed if found by the patriarchy.

Even my grandmother did not like it when I began to try and write my feelings and desires. She never told her history. When I began to write at ten years she said "I have given my life to concealing my feelings, my anger, my despair, now you are going to tell it." And I was.

How great for our children and grandchildren to be able to read this book and know what women were doing and feeling and how wonderful they were.

I am always especially thrilled at such a harvest because it has been written, edited, and published by a community of women, out of isolation, to perceive each other, enlighten and warm the common experience.

It is also a new experience, a new perception of an oppressed generation, now freed to be in their own body, with their own rich imagination and power. Make no mistake — this could not be mistaken for a man's anthology, or for Lord Tennyson, or Byron. Such subjects have not been in patriarchal literature, showing these rich women beings, pitting cherries, singing songs of salads, and sons and empty houses, about places, space of women, and love and loss and children, early morning, dark wounds, mothersong, birth and death, and many most delicate and feminine abysses not spoken of, revealed, or dreamed of in the male establishment.

It is a vivid stream flowing in our culture. I am grateful to these women now. How long it took me through wounds and darkness to know my body and place, to be frank and sing my song!

This book is a song of women together who want to speak to us, touch us, and summon a more rich and creative life.

— Meridel Le Sueur

TABLE OF CONTENTS

ILLUSTRATIONS

ABSORB THE COLORS

SITTING ON THE PORCH

An event, in those days
for which one freshened up.
The houses were close to the street
and to sit on the porch
meant to be accessible,
to visit, chat and receive,
to be public and on display.
My grandmother did not
sit on the porch
before four o'clock
but sometimes stayed there
through sweet summer evenings.
And when I was with her
I thought of it as
an occasion.

IN THIS ENDLESS WHITENESS

In this endless whiteness,
this five-month January of
multi-formed ice:
flat, opaque
solid and shiny
or
in particles so small and blown
they infuse the air, looking like
tangible fog
and quiet —

In this endless whiteness,
sea of faces pale,
drifted with pale hair
subdued, conserving —

Come three sisters,
Plumage shouting
Like tropical birds
Hair shorn
Bodies bursting.
Unexpected exotica
Transplanted from some technicolor
Zone.

No need to yell
"Give it out, sisters!"
They will anyway.

LOOKING SEAWARD

He had stacks of them
and though they must have been soiled,
wrinkled at times,
I picture them coming from the laundry
or fresh from the ironing woman's board,
crisp and folded,
in drawers, on shelves,
thin blue and white stripes,
pales, whites,
short sleeves and long.

The most special were
the tucked-front dress shirts,
their bosoms starched, their bodies soft,
white on white,
broad tucks with stiff collars
imposing in character,
fine tucks on soft batiste,
wide-cuffed, frivolous ruffled fronts,
Daddy wore them all.

At the shore we shirted women
sit in a time line,
my mother, me, my daughters,
his tiny initials faded
but still legible inside our collars.

It is twenty years since
his flesh shrank on his frame,
he yellowed
and died.

TIN

Meetings,
hurried, barricaded at both ends.
Little clumps of minutes spread out
over ten years,
sometimes counted in hours
almost never in days.

There was a time near the globe fountain
- frozen in winter -
you were not well,
and suffering from a panic of loneliness,
asking questions, fast, unanswerable
eyes darting.
And another time
at the January Bar
where, it was whispered,
they took me for a hooker.
Still another, when, walking briefly,
we saw huge teeth
in a curio window.
Meetings where numbness set in so fast
it almost swallowed anticipation.

There is no sequence,
no order in this remembrance.
I cannot name the years
and the seasons, still clear,
arrive in unnumbered lots;
two springs together,
three winters ...
And summers.
Were there ever summers?
Lake-filled and green?

And yet, we never met
- not once -
by accident.

To what does this
fragmented constancy attest?
Can it really be said
we were together a decade,
or should we ignore the lapsing of days,
add up the minutes
and call it a month in the country.

(untitled)

In the middle age
the loss of anarchy is
a hedge against a too-short tomorrow.
The singer says
"still crazy after all these years"
but it's a dragged down, tired out
madness with fear and caution in it.
We're safety crazed.
Smash-the-future-take-it-now
twitches in some distant corner
lived by someone else,
its epiphanies lived by them too.
We reach
with tentative hands
only to run into our own
bricks and mortar,
the future too short to fritter.

November moon
    swift-running river slides dark bands
    past our bench
    cliffs are ghostly
    dead elms lift white branches high

You are silent
I smell musky wet leaves on the path

We see it at the same time
    a deer swims downstream with eyes gleaming
    neck aloft
    calm, purposeful in the middle of the river
    it looks once our way
    a stare secretive, wild
    includes us in a world of woods and water

I remember your story, how you
    sang from a tree above ripe blueberry bushes
    sang freely a wordless song in a powerful voice
    and a deer came to you
    answering your call

PORTRAIT

Little Lavina they called you
distinguished you from Big Lavina
she was small, you were large
until you shrank gradually in the rest home

You were the plain daughter, your mother said
Eva, the pretty one
wits and energy made up for that
never afraid to improvise what you didn't know

You delivered a hundred babies in Medo Township
when the doctor left, you fought on
blood pooling under the bed
and saved mother and child

You lived on the prairie all your life
looking east at the great sky
you saw Norway's mountains
told of Ivar's forbidden fiddling
the time a rival rolled John the Peddler
down the hill into Ingeborg's farmyard
and they married

In the picture, you and Knute stand together
in the hard-scrabbled yard by
blooming apple trees
you hold blossoms in your hand

THE CHECKERBOARD LOUNGE

Magic Slim snakes across his steel-strings
    a delta moan slow as a hot summer night:

        Listen, my woman's gone
        Yeah, she's done gone far 'way
        m-m-m, my woman's gone
        To love some other man

Junior Wells sits at the bar, back to us, nursing a Bud
    Hey Junior, how 'bout sittin' in on this one?
    the frat boys at the long table go wild
    stomping till Junior undulates to the mike
    straw hat cocked, skinny red shirt hanging to his knees

Junior sings
    pain too strong, too fresh to be a lament
    his harp playing raw, charged
    a glissando becomes a scream
    a quaver a sob
    the notes bend, break, spill to the floor
    we pick them up
    we who cannot cry

NINETEEN-FIFTY-TWO

Sugar bread at Uncle George's
Games on Madge Wasgatt's porch
March for "Ike," fall off the bike
Stain the pink silk scarf

Mother playing "Malagueña"
I dance madly
Dervish whirling toward the bay

Patent shoes with vaseline
"Fairy's Harp" left hand crossed over
"Snow White" at the matinee

Pralines sweet in dark New Orleans
Pink motels' metallic water
Cotton shacks, TV antennas
Mammy cushion voodoo doll

Sugar bread at Uncle George's
Morning-glories, mourning dove

QUARTET FOR THE END OF TIME

Straining against the taut string
    through the ascension
    and slow falling away
    with pounding blood
    throat's fullness

I play the flower in light rain
    the blackbird at daybreak
    the angel of the apocalypse
    with tangled rainbow hair

Together, we unfold the eternal song
Over blue-orange chords of paradise

LET THE CHILD BE

"Let the child be, Etta!
She wants to see the axing
    of the meat she'll eat today!"
And so the child did see
    the wonders of a beheaded rooster
    tearing around the barnyard.

"Let the child be, Henry!
She wants to see the birthing
    of the kittens with whom she'll play."
And so the child did see
    the wonders of a patient feline
    bearing four wet, blind cats.

"Let the child be, Etta!
She wants to see the milking
    of the cows she fondles each day."
And so the child did see
    the wonders of Gramp's hands
    pulling out Bossie's white milk.

"Let the child be, Henry!
She wants to see the pulling
    of the vegetables planted in May."
And so the child did see
    the wonders of delicious roots
    yielding to Grammie's firm tug.

The child did "be," she did "see"
All of her fifth summer
    with Henry and Henry's Etta.
And so the child, grown woman today,
    ponders about grandparents'
    nurturing, unconditional love.

PROMETHEA

Bound breathless in early green
adorned with golden beads
you are destined in dark quiet
to wait out your mystery.

A season for everything:
    wind turns,
    frost tests,
    rains toss,
you season your seasons
    helpless in your silken shell,
tiny puppet.

You can not know many Mays have passed.
Xochipilli has born other secret ones
    to his Madonna's breast.
She rocks them as her own!

Your Flower Prince brings another Mayspring.
Light penetrates your dark chrysalis!
You bleed red rain,
bindings dissolve,
you emerge
Promethea!

24/30   Demeter   © Rikki 1979

TO TOUCH THE HAND OF THE POET
to Kathleen Wiegner

You read in poet's fashion
A monotonous drone, low, soft
Punctuated with raised eyebrow
And breaks of explanation

I see your round eyes
Tunnels to your soul
Drop often - to hide
Pain.

You roll a silver dollar
On your tongue,
Spit out black sunshine
On meat that goes bad in a day.

I hear your number, three,
You Christine and
Whoever makes your story
Sad.

You charge the birth
Should be from the sea
Casting up children at our feet
With seaweed in their hair.

I touch your thin hand
That has written a
Million miles and
Held two million fires.

My Sabbath today!
Some insist, "Must be Sunday!"
Others, "Saturday!"
But my body says, "Today!"
    Sandy Ego

'Tis my day to rest
And do the most pleasant things.
So I taste the best
Rhubarb sauce with toastlings.

I smell apple trees
Release posh-pink petals.
Strewing flower-confetti
The whimsical breezes settle.

I hear yellow bird
Warble glorious music,
Knowing he'll be heard
By her, eating thistle bics.

I touch him who comes home.
He presses his lips to mine.
Laugh together, we two alone,
Deep rushes ruby love wine.

I smile at high blue sky,
And deeply breathe in spring.
My day to rest, aye,
And do the most pleasant things.

SONG OF SALADS
(as sung by mother and daughter-in-law)

*Confused is the man
whose mother is a saint, and
whose mate is a poet!*

Sandy Ego

Her salads were perfection!
Cabbage, carrots, pineapple
jelled into shapely forms
of lemon amber
by hands
used to serve.

I dare toss my greens
high and free
with fruits of passion
spiced with rare season
into crystal bowls.

Prized salads in peril,
she offered,
"Take my mold.
Fill it with my recipe.
Share it with him
whom we will serve.
I mean
serve it to him
whom we will share."

He got fat eating salads.

FLOWERS

You would bring me flowers
Now and then
One yellow rose
You knew my favorite.
I would strip just enough leaves
To fit in the thin vase
Placing it next to our bed
Changing the water often enough
To keep it alive for days
Then, no matter my ministrations
The flower would turn brown and brittle.
I let it dry right there in our room
Removing it only encircled in dust.

The roses came no more
After we dug Jesse's grave
In the backyard where we could watch over her
I would bring her colorful carnations
Every day then every two
But you said people might not want
To buy the house
With Jesse's dirt mound and jar of flowers
So I took the last bunch
Just before they totally rotted
And pelted them down the steep hill beyond
Where they fell inert.
The house still hasn't sold.

TENSE

You
Certainly
Made it easier
For me
To write about you.
No longer
Must I wrestle
With awkward tenses
Now
All I have
Are Passed.

TAPS

They ushered me into the residents' lounge
Apologized   there was no other place for me
The special speaker

Two old men were there
One asleep in a chair he had been in forever
I watched his stomach   still alive
I'd been warned
He sometimes undressed in public
The other tapped a flimsy cane
Dum   Da Da   Dum Dum
Was it code
Or hope

Soon a young nurse appeared
Shouted
Robert
Do you have to go to the bathroom
Huh   Robert
Tap tap   They sparred
His rugged silence   Tap tap
Her sing-song shout   Dum Dum
Off they went

Dum Dum   Tap Tap

TODAY IS MY DAY

As I awoke
The sun cheerily poked
Its head into my window
Announced
Wake Up   Wake
Up   Today is your day.
  Once I built a railroad
Today is my day
Who were you making love
To last night
As your eyes closed tight and teared?
  I made it run
I never know your thoughts anymore
Why do you keep telling
Me it will be all right soon?
  I made it race against time
That I won't die
Ever?
No never!
  Once I built a railroad
TODAY IS MY DAY
Who was that lover
  And now it's done
TODAY IS MY DAY
TODAY IS MY DAY
And now it's done
Ever!

BASS LICKS

They give me eight bars
Here and there
Eyes close   hips in heat
Bass licks.
The folks watching
Cheer me louder than anyone
Then I open my eyes slow
      smile shy
And kick it back to the lead.
People stomp their feet
      clap their hands
As we go longer   harder
My guitar throbs quicker and louder
Someone up front beats her hands
      on her knees
In time with my picks and slides
They mix my voice low
The mike's just for show
On and on we go
A perpetual motion machine
Until it's real late
We pack it up
And then I wonder
When the cancer's coming back.

unlike the nautilus

unlike the nautilus or the hermit-crab
        never able to pull out of the body
too close to the blood and bone
stuck in this flesh
        while the neighborhood goes downhill
        paint peeling   mortar crumbling
in what was once
an impressive example of domestic architecture

what else then
but these eyes   needing a stronger lens
        straining to focus the fine print
these teeth   capped and crowned
        a little wobbly in their sockets
        wincing at too much sweetness
                to slide into the ripe juice of pears
these unwilling muscles   unable even to sin
        about ready for the holy oils

but the nose still has its knowledge
sure of the reek of the clam flats
        the sharp salt of incoming tides
        the fresh scent of the fog
and no stiffening joints hinder the tongue

having no other home   I'll be here
till the ramshackle frame falls down

in the zone of the interior

day after day the great spatterware canners
sat rocking and steaming on the two gas stoves

Lula walked back and forth carrying kettles
across the gray and green geometry of the linoleum
scrubbing and boiling jars   matching lids

the sweat trickled down our faces   behind my ears
we sat at the kitchen table cutting corn off the cob
stringing beans   peeling tomatoes   shelling peas
crisp   brilliant as jade   sweet to the tongue
so pale and faded come January

my mother   surrounded by county extension pamphlets
considered vitamins   nutrition   and calories
planned her strategy to out-flank a garden
always trying to grow faster and faster
filled the storerooms with pints and quarts
that cast their winter between me and the spring
wasted nothing
would defeat the Germans   the Japanese   and the weather
once I think I pitted cherries for two weeks
and the little finches in the lilacs learned to fly

I remember that I watched my grandmother
decorate the corn with strips of red pimento
silently simmer plain sauce into apple butter
just because I liked it
fill a shelf with the jewels of watermelon pickle
the glow of clear jellies   ruby and topaz
and make sinful brandied peaches

every summer day   not a sharp word spoken
in that struggle between beauty and use
her sugar coupons politely offered   politely refused
in a war without quarter

winter night

out in the barn at midnight
I have stood by the laboring mother
    breathing with her breathing   muscles contracting
    to help her cast her burden
        up onto the beachhead of this world
how tenderly we gaze back
into the solemn infant's stare
    as life keeps promising and promising

I listen to the raging winter wind
    baffled and wild at walls and windows
till I rock in the ceaseless cradle of the seasons
dragged by the swift momentum of the sun and moon
    at the tumbling planet's chariot wheel
the snow lies deep and cold
where pastures were and will be velvet-soft
and life keeps breaking oaths and making new ones
    just an old soak on yet another bitter morning
we hear each other's cries
and know our flesh is one with the bird on the wing
    and the fox in the trap

swept away

almost before the current seized me
I began to ask

will I figure out how to let myself float
drift   into eddying pools
say yes to the rush
        so many feet of fall to the mile?

can I chart a course when I know
the swift run downriver
how even the quietest reach of water
cannot be contained
        the day the ice goes out?

and if these moments flash by
quick minnows
        sliding away from my fingers
I'll carry the flood with me everywhere
        will that be enough?

Alice's trip to the fair

hooked on the ride
through glittering mirrors   calliope tunes
rollercoaster excitement
swinging from the tips of your fingers
on around the curve of your hip
in and out
    of the mysterious cave of Eleusis
the swift screaming stoop from the sky
and climbing the air
    back up to the peak of the mountain
coming to hang exhausted in your arms
    asleep inside the gates
awakened at dawn
to thoughts about times and seasons
never wanting to strike the bright tents
    asking to live in the park

sonnet to nature

you cut and sow again. you send
the birds into the morning skies.
what can it be to you if one of a thousand cries
and falls before you have proclaimed its end?

you light the blue night's body, and you wander
across the earth in every shape the seasons will express.
your breath laughs at the ice, and in the fall you squander
the fortune of your brilliant success.

o take me back. the peaceful shore
gladly absorbs the last wave of the sea.
your lives are transformations without number,

you will not envy the forgetful slumber
of one who's fallen out of gravity
into a world that reaches yours no more.

learning how to say goodbye

take the bridges, for instance;
their assertion of relative eternity
as they frame the trembling sunsets with black arches.

the way they lift from the waters
patterns of changing visions,
themselves unchanging,

and watch the Mississippi take along
the memory of parks and power plants and houses
and different kinds of banks,

the beds of shrubbery, the steep
majestic cliffs - forever, or at least
for one short span of life.

the sandstone will outlast countless goodbyes -
and yet I feel: the match
that lit its beauty was your presence,

your hand, so small by contrast,
so immense by meaning, the frame
that brought the details of the city's atmosphere to life.

like the river, I say,
back on the bridge,
moving across its shadow on the waters,

the river with its many films
of images, and all must go, and all are kept
in some deep layer of its endless body -

I will be always here and always leaving.

paradox I

through your
smooth shoulder
to the heart of
the earth glowing
burns
my mouth
its course the mark
of passion

drawn by the black
force from behind
your eyes into
those spaces unknown clear
unending

is that fall
irrevocable
the loss is
dangerous the dive
too deep down out
too far is that
destructive?

my mouth can't tell
where it ends yours begins
but my mind wanders

wind in the trees
the news the ticking
of the clock your shoes next
to the paper
torture you are right
goes on and on
the surface screaming

two thoughts now
lost shall
emerge
too much of us
in the world not
to want return

paradox II

I am the time,
Now flowing from the core
Into the world.

The wave whose circle claims
The growing circles
Of the sea.

*

Do not resist the tide;
If it takes everything, then
Everything must go.

Death does not come from outside, you
Will still be there when pain
Has washed you clean.

I cursed the second when the last leaf
Fell.
Cried over my own end.

No violence done.
The turning point is when you feel
The moment enter you.

*

I am the breath through which the world
Expands its waves.

I am the time now, flowing
From the core.

good-bye in an empty house
or: a lesson to the shirts

I. the house was empty.
   like the tea cup on the piano, forgotten
   but with the residue of what filled the atmosphere before
   silence had settled on the furniture.

   disconnected
   bare walls leading,
   now and then, to a corner of human settlement:
   your blanket, the summer pictures, dried out flowers
   on the table.

   room after room repeated it;
   your presence would not change
   the loneliness in this house.

II. then I saw your shirts in the closet - good grief!
    as I shook hands with them, I realized
    their miserable state: no countenance,
    just hanging around,
    deflated.

    I said: shape up! don't let yourselves go.
    there are other people to hang on to,
    same size, and most probably
    less hard on you than the guy who is presently wearing you
    out.

    while I was lecturing them, the radio went on by itself,
    to wake you up. those mindless things
    miss the big changes.

III. it started raining.
     I used your shower and drank your tea.
     fortunately, you don't know what I owe you beyond that.

     where I come from, the houses are different. prisons,
     but gentle. every inch of you
     inhabited by someone's thoughts.

     while in this jungle of forces to whom you don't matter,
     the choice was: be free or be lost.
     so I was free.

     in the kitchen, I tried a few steps for a new dance,
     collected my belongings and went to the party.
     I think I left nothing behind.

TAKING FLIGHT
(For Theona)

Angel-hair,
high cheek bones,
birch frame.
Eyes — clear as a bird's,
voice
with time behind it.

I see you jump high
on the trampoline,
almost a grandma then
and still full of marvel
as my child finds
an empty snake-skin
at the edge
of your wild-flowers.

Seems just a breath ago —
I don't know how it all
rushed upon us,
although the pain
must have been eons
and the thrust-upon weakness
a rage.

While you moved
your household
more often than I ever could,
my garden hosted
your lady-slippers.
I returned them this spring.

How did you manage
to plant more gardens?

I did not come
to see you, broken —
I was afraid
of a spirit, gone
from its shell.

My mind has framed you
mid-air,
arms flung out for balance
and you
taking flight.

46

47

OLD WORLD

My blood hums
to the swell of the land,
my flesh vibrates
on the endless ladder
of the train
that rung by rung
reaches my childhood.

Each crumb of the earth
is one of my cells
recycled
from dreams.
Well-known vignettes
shutter
through pupils,
old films brought to light.

Winding streets,
squares with tear-fountains,
statues of wishes
unfold
accordion-fashion,
flash back into the mind.

Along the veins
of the rivers
and small brook capillaries
I rush past weeds
of summer days
taller than I was.

In the mountains
I get off.
The air rinses my eyes,
colors burn bright on the iris:
This is my blue cradle,
the rock matrix.
As I lie down
spread-eagled
it sings a low welcome.

ALTWEIBERSOMMER*

When Grossmutter talked,
family history
rolled by loaded high
like a wood field wagon.
Homespun names and kinship
knit an intricate pattern.

While I played and overheard her
spinning yarn
with an old-time gossip,
my ear attuned itself
to marriages,
to each year's Kirmess-dance,
the fistfights like rituals
and three-day wakes.
They unravelled crossed and tangled strands.

And though I was bored then:
tedious litany,
alliances of second cousins,
forgotten maiden names —
wind-woven threads, *Altweibersommer*
always the hands working,

how I miss it passing my ears
like a rosary turned lullaby.

*Austrian expression for Indian summer and also for long spiderweb-threads floating in
the autumn air.

CHINOOK

Not one rock
to lean over
and obstruct
this long breath
of a continent,
open like a careless palm.

From the valley bottom,
snug as a kettle,
I have come this far.

I hang on the clothes line,
get to the barn
and hand over hand
move back into the house.
My father once gave me
a bright doll on a rope.

Outside
the big grunts
of the wind-sow
reach for my door.
I dream of blue rocks.
Like prairie grass
my nerves bend low
and the small twigs
of my brain
snap off.

ON THE WIND
(For Hanno)

You tend the flowers
as always,
watch their first shoots,
give care.

Your voice steady,
your white hair
stronger than grief
flows on the wind.

But your eyes
betray a sheen,
they are on the trip
ahead
they see the still form
pulled
from the lake,
the white hyacinth —
your son.

We see you
to the airport.
Your strength is rock.
Only in the close hug
can I feel your interior land
slide.

NICHOLAS AT ONE YEAR

All winter,
we've carried you and your spirit under the sleeping trees
and the evergreens visiting from another world.
Old rhymes flurry into us,
the most powerful reason
counting for nothing at all.
For a time, you were very sick. You lay still.
You cried out, from your fierce hot mind.

When you were born, the contractions stopped.
Nicholas, peace
comes from far off, like pepper, like viruses
and light. How grievous to come to earth!
Someday, you might be a traveler

in a country at war, no more or less luminous
than the others. If I could open the door
in your shadow, I would see you grown —
rotating oranges in your hands,
shoveling the white snow up into hills,
knowing the names of the muscles
that hold everyone up.

A year was forever once.
The night of your first birthday,
you were given a tambourine.
The three of us were alone, trying to be
family. There weren't any footprints.
No one came to us with sweets or rest.

How can I tell you this story?
It is a story strung with electricity,
where the apartment is cockleburrs on brittle stalks.
The baby painstakingly picks the noodles from his tray.
Air rasps in and out of the parents, wanting
every year to end.

Is the fighting in the story thirst or deep river?
The fighting will make us forever sleepless.
You were a year old.

The ones God made you with were angry.
I took you and rushed — you, laughing and shining —
into the bitter cold. Snow took
to the air, the blind, the everlasting snow.
The fir trees scattered
needles into drifts.
You had just learned how to clap your hands,
and, in the way of one-year-olds,
to open and close, open and close them

goodbye.

VIBORG, SOUTH DAKOTA
August 1934

I know about the other house, the house
under this one, almost as dark.
The floors are strewn with lace collars
and black shoes. I know how dirt turns its back
on the bedroom mirror, how chips of glass
pace the hall.

I've got new names: orphan, little piano
out of tune, prairie rose torn on a barbed fence.

My aunts have come here to pack up
all the clothes. They can't hear the dresses
call out to me, or the trousers, still fretting
over what's to be done. My aunts say

Lois, there aren't any meadowlarks
trapped in the kitchen.
Lois, your Mama didn't forget her shadow
on your bed.
They tell me Papa's arms aren't pushing
through the weeds in the yard.

I hate the teeth marks on this pencil.
I want to forget what dying is: a wet sheet nailed
over the west window, clouds sifting down
like veils of lies.

At the bottom of the creek, my baby
is sleeping between the stones. I've never seen her.
Her cries turn into thin sticks
and float downstream. She's what became

of the braid I cut off that day, the clatter
when I threw the scissors in, the terrible scolding
no one was there to make.

BERTRAND, NEBRASKA
29 April 1978

My uncles told me to grab onto the front part
of the coffin. There almost isn't enough room
for my hand and it looks blue,
like it doesn't belong to me anymore.
He feels so light. They don't need this many boys
to carry him.

I was glad when the man from the furniture store
closed the lid. That was the worst part.
Grandpa has on a black robe just like the preacher's
and an awful collar glued to his neck.
The doctors must have made him wear those clothes.
I never saw them before. He must have been
wearing those clothes when he died.

Mother stopped walking. I had to pull her away
because I could tell she was about to call
him daddy again, in front of all these strangers.
It was like pulling a crooked person.
Everyone said a prayer I never heard before without
even looking at their books. The church is full
of people with red books. They won't look at them.
Some of the people don't want to sing.
The song sounds strange. It sounds bad.

Now a man with a straw hat is telling me
my grandpa christened him. He's shaking my hand.
I don't know what he means. We're about to have
a big lunch. Old ladies are coming in with napkins
and bowls of jello. They keep asking me my name.
They keep guessing I'm someone else's boy.

WHILE YOU WERE GONE,
THE CHAIRS OUTSIDE THE NEXT HOUSE

The bridge we're walking, suspended on breath
and paint, is no place to want anything.
We do.
It's becoming something else.
Meanwhile, we're trying to make sentences
for each other:
badly, taken, love, you.
Lamps don't wake up inside ordinary jars.
We are not unhappy.

Downstairs, nothing is colored
the familiar way, or lives there
with its own noise. We're two rooms
blown in from the house that used to stand here,
nailed to a strange closet of letters
and changed luck. With persistence, our sorrows

have become aloof, private as the geese
on the snow that night, the way they burst into flame
when they tucked their heads under their wings.
Our skates pulled us like mute curtains
across the lake, the ice splintering into coins
we didn't pick up. You went in.

Out here was like loving you.
I wanted to introduce you to the family
standing in the kitchen of the next house.
Out on the lawn, their chairs
were very still.
You never saw them. The chairs
were part of the grief
of that hour when the street plummets
through the trees, the worst kind of star,
when windows light up their indefinite dreams,
when the chairs admit they were left out there
for a reason.

The day you went to prison was like the day you came back.
You dried your hair with a towel.
Douglas, you buttoned your old shirt.
You used both hands.

STARS
"O Look at all the fire-folk sitting in the air!"
                                                    Hopkins

In the country where I grew, white-breasted birds
are flying through the cottonwoods, over fields
of yellow corn wrapped in husks. Twilight,

fireflies spark over cattails in the marsh.
I am writing by hand. Pins hold the thought
to its telling. I am writing by hand

because we are often gloomy and afraid, and we need
homemade words to go on, promise and companions
to house us in the world.

Martha says stars are like the light you see
when you look up through a colander. She's busy
with fleece: skeins of black wool, then

a triangular cap, flecked white. The spinning wheel
whirs. Needles click and tat-a-tat. Some stars fall
onto her skirt. If you look up, you can see

brilliant broken crockery in God's hand.
Newborns are fire-folk, I think, begun long ago
like starlight, mute, wise, and full of wishes

to be granted. In autumn, Martha was away a season
picking apples. She promised rocking for my
secret child. I tied an apron over my stomach

and sliced peppers. The orchards lost
their red planets. Snow spun out of heaven.
When day went dark,

Martha came in from the wind
wearing her handmade stars.

SAN VITALE, BOLOGNA

The mosaics on the walls
carry the centuries with dignity,
fading into the rust-browns
of earth. Carved out of rock,
this chapel is a cave
of reverence, a dance to
the nymphs of the peninsula.

Only when the indoor lights
go out,
do the reds and golds
of the elongated windows
flash their abstract beauty
across the stone floor.

ELEGY FOR A CITY

In Venice
soft green carpets support the buildings
yielding to the waters
that cradle them. Holidaymakers
turn the streets into
a world of orgy. Each delays the retreat
indoors, shops refuse to close.

The ferryboats
continue to carry full loads
of passengers the length of the main canal
throughout the night. The crowds
on the bridge use time exposures
to imprint for posterity
the artificial lights playing on the water.

When the darkness
captures the city, the black
gondolas will sneak through
the smaller waterways, the songs
of the boatmen echoing
like the sound
of church bells from the mainland.

PRAYER OF A NEOPHYTE

Standing before the *David*,
I struggle to block out the lens
of your camera. You focus on objects
highlighted in the *Michelin*. The rough,
blurred outlines of this *Pieta*
must disintegrate under such scrutiny.
The broad unformed mask of the woman
would become a cliff,
emerging virginal from the waters.

Each day I have half-listened
to the facts you share, pausing
at the second level of the half-surrendered
Coliseum
to wonder what choices remained.
Animals numbering nine hundred
(or was it nine thousand)
died the first week of the inauguration
while the crowds cheered. Today
both animals and people
are transformed into limestone,

magnify the light of the sun
darkening the blood walls
of the Palatine. You and I moved
further, into the grounds of the Forum,
where trees were encroaching
upon the ruins. I became a Vestal Virgin,
my ossification merging
with the decapitated figure standing fifth
from the end of the row. I felt
your accusing eyes but caught

in the passageway between house
and temple without a head, I could not
speak to you. If I had I would say,
the trees of Rome stand like artists' shapes
against an invisible canvas. In Sienna,
this would have been impossible
for the medieval lords, trapped
by their belief that language
differed little from the morsecode

clatter of carriages over cobblestones,
built to shut out nature, crowding
the houses so that they could not breathe
and come to life, connecting them
with concrete squares, and drawing flowers
on the walls, to remind the peasants
of pink dragons
that once played with their children
by the seaside.

I love language, too.
For example, the *David* confronting me.
Note how the sculptor sections the torso,
the upperchest, thick yet pliable
with the muscles extending down the upper arm
but stopping short of the elbow. The rib-cage,
median in size, yet obviously
the center of strength and balance. The haunches
of the figure slender and sinewy

to emphasize the fullness
of the thigh muscles. And then, after all
that, surprising us with the face, young
and ionian, like a neophyte calmly transcending
the mystery of his vision. Today,
the mosaic women in the Palatine begin
to come to life,
to inhabit my brain carrying vessels held
at a careful distance

from their silk gowns. As the colors
brightened, they made me blind for a moment,
urging that I listen only
to the music caught in the instant.
This was their reward
for my pilgramages. I had prayed at the tombs,
begging the one-time possessors
of those splinters of bone to lead me
beyond syntax, into the silence

of the blue madonnas
with their bodies cradled on grass,
into the eloquence
of the young bodies of Florence
perfected in stone.

ARES

This is not the god of war
we know today, this quiet figure
with the pensive human face.

The limbs sport no
angularity, the flesh
no curves that define motion.

No doubt, the battle was a draw,
it not being clear on which side
the writhing bodies belonged.

Had the god stayed
away from Olympus too long,
forgetting the taste of nectar?

For twenty centuries now
he has been forced to listen to
the insistent revolution of the earth.

He has shut out the clang
of iron against flesh
by rooting himself in stone.

AUTISTIC BOY IN THE LIBRARY

Inside you there is a world
I can not reach
when fish became birds,
and dinosaurs trampled huge ferns,
when scream and squawk named names,
and there were no words.

Your hands tell some words
hurt, hurt, hurt you sign at me
and show your cuticles torn into shreds.
What is it you tried to say
before you ripped your skin like paper?
You reach out, touch my hair
touch yours.

Somehow you know fish and you know bird.
You sign them now the same
again and again, swim and fly
your hands through air
as if it were water.
You show me you have a new shirt,
you show me book-bird-fish,
you mean business now, you are here for book.

You jump up from your chair,
sign hurt and a sudden red,
dart to blank television screen
and stare at your shadowy face.
Do you wonder if you are inside
that box and your body?
Have you seen today's war
and heard the count of the dead?

Your business here is not what I thought.
Can you find that genesis of fish and bird?
Can be begin once more in that time of no-names?
Can we find peace without flash-bang bombs?
Can your fingers move you into book and fish and bird
and happy-please without hurt?

SEED CATALOGS IN JANUARY

Unable to remember summer, I lurch on ice
plod through ragged drifts
to the mailbox held up by snow and dumb luck
surrounded by the sound of snowblowers
I try to picture a calico cat
in the gingko tree, fan-shaped leaves
stirring the wind above the astilbe in July.

Zipped into my son's jacket
I stuff my hands into his pockets
I do not want to find only letters today
I want this black cave of metal
to open to a seed catalog
I want round pumpkins and Hubbard squash
orange marigolds and red salvia
purple cabbage, eggplant and kohlrabi
I want the poetry of radishes: Pax, Inca
French breakfast, Easter egg, almost burpless
Inside my mittens, my fingers
itch to touch Belamcandia, Browallia,
Alstromeria, Caelceolaria, and my nose
sniffs out new allergies.

All the way back up the drive I search
out places for Big Boy and Early Girl
Kandy Korn, Yellow Doll, and Sugar Ann Snap
I lean into Cinneraria and Celosia
decide this summer for maybe-sure we'll plant
heather and lavendar, morning glories
and clematis - border everything with purple petunias

Inside again, the seed catalog on the table
I sip coffee and check the bird book
Come April the heron flies over that first
freedom of crocus.

3/25   Persephone   Riki © 1980

THE OLD WOMAN REMEMBERS

Why do you ask? Of course I lie
it is too soon for truth or too late
I do not know.
When I take out my teeth each night and
look at my mouth, sunk deep like a sand pit
and take off this black wig
I see what is left — grey thin hair.
That, my young friend, is truth.
I do not like it. Why should you?
You hang on my every word
a child. Learning to walk you hung on
went around the edge of the room
time after time. You did not see
all the room in the center.
The center is far from the edge
to get there, you let yourself go
move away from the familiar.
So, I lie. Talk about the edge
make it sound the center
and you listen over tea
your eyes full of tears clear as spring rain
I tell you what you want to hear
seventy years ago my brother died
I washed his body green wood and willow.
My father came back from the war
sat near the window looked at his son's grave
cursed me for singing.
I do not tell you of Paris and love and wine
and red shoes. Nor of my days in the chorus
and nights on stage in Berlin living out of a trunk
with room for hangers and four drawers
moving on schedule to applause
and the young men. These are my secrets
and only I am left now to remember the touch
flesh on flesh silk against my skin
that sudden wind of cut grass and lilacs
and sand against my back

a hand with dark black hair on the fingers
pulling me to a small house with finches
violets and a garden
nor the baby with brown eyes who died
before she laughed
and the years of looking for her smile
at the bottom of bottles.
You want to hear about my life
I tell you what I choose.
You feel trapped today on the second
floor of marriage
caught between childhood and responsibility
You move from the edge to the center
find that early life of your parents' love
in your bed each night.
I no longer listen. What I tell you
may be from the TV or from a story
someone told me in a language you will never hear.
Like an old album, I hold pictures I do not recall
nameless faces in front of Crazy Ludwig's castle.
My lie is not the past
there is much paper telling that truth.
At least, the past is not my biggest lie.
I tell you things will get better.
The truth is they change.

MY SON BRINGS BUTTERFLIES

Light yellow wings pinched tight
between his small thumb and forefinger

The color of new leaves
Petals that hold spring wind forever still
Bits of October cornhusks tossed by the wind

Caged in glass they beat invisible boundaries
Bruised, on the bottom, lie broken pieces of the moon

Next to me at night your body flutters
Dreams I can not share and you will not remember
Rising, I move quick against the darkness
Above the lamp a soft yellow triangle brushes the wall
Fine as powder the dark sifts through me

Butterflies caught before supper are still now
Soft triangles, silent as dead love

LISTENING TO VOICES

This fantasy comes
when the phone rings
that when I answer
the voice on the other end will say
This is your dream poet.

Or when opening the door
in response to loud rapping
he will be standing there
white hair flying
and he will say
I've come.

Or when stacking wood
I hear leaves crackle
he stands tall above me
red scarf fluttering
and I say
Did you bring that woman with you?
And he looking at me will say
Certainly you must live here with some man!

I pile wood beside the stove
put another piece on the fire
and walk slowly to my room
I read again
There are women we love whom we never see . . .

DRIVING HOME AFTER LUNCH WITH JEAN

Our voices rise and fall
in a room full of people
we do not see or hear
our heads come together
then move apart as in some strange ritual
handed down
from a mother culture
long forgotten
or never recognized

she rises and is gone
I sip my now cool coffee
examine the emptiness
across from me
talk echoes in my head

I put a 25¢ tip by my plate
although I can never
get rye krisp with my soup
I go to the library
find Kabir
carry him to my car
he rides quietly beside me
an acceptable lover

but somehow inside
I am not quiet
Kabir says
"if you had to cut off your head
and give it to someone
what difference would it make?"

sunflowers nod at me
from the edge of the freeway
seed spilled last fall
swallows congregate

foolishly in the road
scatter as I approach
in the rear view mirror
one remains on the pavement
wing strangely askew

"and the only woman awake
is the woman who
has heard the flute"
I do not want to sleep
play for me.

THE IDES OF MARCH
(for Gerald Stern)

Later today when most of the snow is melted
and the yard is brown again, she'll stand for one minute
at the front door, forehead pressed on cool glass.
She'll start thinking about the garden
and the tulips on the west side of the house
and how the dogwood will grow again
and how the lilac will smell in blossom.
She will live in the light
as if she belonged
as if the children were there
as if her heart were
and she were floating somewhere in space
as if she were in Norway
walking beside fish nets
touching their fiber toughness
smelling the huge catch they held
going down to the wooden houses and tiny boats
on the clear fjord.

MINDCARVER

Don't recall his death now.
Alone in Yankton, rigid
back arched, eyes open
needing someone to close lids
relax hands.
Hands that held shovel
made mouth organ say
Remember me, remember me.

Don't think of him at home all the time
liquid blue eyes apologetic
pleading, his breath
reeking of beer, snoose.

Think of him as one who left his home
a child of eight to herd sheep
on a lonely Norwegian island
no mother to take care.

Think of him as the man in the brown photo
hand curled around daughter's face
in Vermillion, holding hands
with your brother.
Keep his hands holding
or crossed on his chest
or akimbo on slim hips
your father's hands before you were born.

IN PRAISE OF EARLY MORNINGS
IN PRAISE OF SMALL TOWNS

I close the back door
quietly on the house
leave behind its light
its warmth
walk into the street
under Venus bright
in the southeast
I run up the hill
snow along the street
shoulder height
two snowstorms back to back
a black and yellow bike
abandoned in a drift
startles me as I
round a corner
packed snow glares
in the street light
I hug the side
where loose snow
under my weight
scrunches
I run the width of the town
four blocks north
one east
four blocks south
back and forth
on the lower main street
a traffic jam
two cars have stopped
in front of the post office
Mr. Voth is depositing
his wife Sammy
at the restaurant
she will open at six
out of the dark pickup cab
she smiles at me

up at this hour for no good reason
down the next block I walk
on the straight stretch home
George greets me
on the way to his grocery store
how are you he says
I am fine
in this crisp dark air
in this small town
I am not afraid
where all is mine
my private running field
at this small hour
I am fine

DINOSAUR SPRING

A violet wash is streaked across the clouds.
Triceratops, Brachiosaurus, Trachodon
browse the high greenery, heave through
the dissipating mists.
They are as vacant as we are:
They don't see how mountains are growing,
how flowers change spring by spring,
how feathers form.

Last night I walked among the dinosaurs,
hardly taller than a claw.
I touched their feet with my fingertips,
my tongue numb with wonder.

At seven this morning two mallards
and a pair of Canada geese
preened themselves in the light of the pond.
Awake on a morning like this one,
jays screeching from treetop to fencepost,
I have to strain to imagine
how people wake up
in San Salvador, Johannesburg, Beirut.
The background roar grows louder,
a neighbor screams for her child.

Just now I took my baby out of his crib
and teetered on the edge of the vortex.
I saw millions of hands imploring,
mouths open, eyes his.
I fell into a universe of black, starry water,
and through that into monstrous love
that wants to make the world right.

I can comfort my son:
The ghost in the closet, the foot-eating fish
on the floor can be washed away
with a hug and a tumbler of milk.
But the faceless face? The nuclear piñata
over our heads? The bone finger pointing?

Through the window I see the sky
that hung over the dinosaurs.
The flight of a grackle catches my eye
and pulls it down toward the moving water.
I can't see the larger motion, leaves
mouldering into new soil.
If I lay on my back in the yard,
I'd feel how we're hanging on
to this planet, attached even to her
by the sheer luck of gravity.

I have to shake my head, I've grown so solemn.
It's my turn to vacuum the house.
In the din, I go back to my dream:
Holding my son by the hand,
I walk again among the dinosaurs.
In by breast my heart pours and pours
so that it terrifies me, pours and pours out
its fathomless love, like the salt mill
at the bottom of the sea.

LIGHT UNDER THE DOOR

I remember hiding in the hall closet,
down with the dust and the extra shoes,
the hems of the big peoples' coats
brushing my uppermost braids. Daddy was coming.
I could tell from the crunch of wheels,
the thunk of the heavy car door,
the rattle of keys at the lock.
His hard soled shoes came toward me,
a voice like Othello's
asked my mother where I was.
I was ready to swoon with delight,
but the footsteps faded,
the voice asked for dinner.

I remember the smell of wool,
the gritty floor under my palms,
the thin light under the door.
My mother stirred, chopped,
opened the oven to check on the cornbread.
I heard her answer my sister
while Daddy went into their bedroom
to take off his Air Force uniform.
Outside, a plane like a buzz saw
sliced the distant sky.

That day in kindergarten
a buzzer went off;
Mrs. Liebel jumped up
and made us hide on the polished floor
under our desks.
Not even the naughtiest boys giggled

as we watched a fly explore
the alphabet over the blackboard
and looked up at wads of petrified gum.
I'm sitting in the closet
waiting for the bomb.

No, that's a lie.
I'm standing here in the kitchen,
a grown up woman, a mother,
with used breasts. Upstairs,
the man I love and our son
are playing. The baby
touches his father's knee,
steps, stops, then runs away
with his off-balance gait.
His father chases him, hooting,
to the table where they stop for breath,
then the baby squeals and takes off
for the other room.

The sun rises in the window over the breakfast table
as I scramble the eggs. On the radio
a pleasant male voice announces yesterday's
disasters. The jays have carried the larger crumbs off,
now they come back for the rest.

My father opened the closet door. A light like a look
into the heart of fire blinded me for a moment:
I didn't see him there.
I remember the good smell of beans and cornbread
and the clash of plates being put on the table.
I remember Mama's voice humming mezzo
as I walked out into the light.

MAMA'S MURDERS

Her leg flew open like a dictionary dropped,
the white fat sickened till her blood
filled the wound and I, dumb with terror,
ran away from the gully guady with broken glass
while my sister's scream shrank to child size
at my cowardly back. A white door opened
as my fists blurred on the wood.
The white lady who took me in
was no age, had no face, only a voice
from somewhere else that asked my mother's name
over the rip of clean sheets.
Jennifer came alone up the forbidden trail,
leaving bloody footprints in the snow.

Five-fifty on a wet October morning.
I'm awake, still running home to get Mama,
confession still cold on my tongue.
I sit up in the dark. I count my murders.
A crow calls from the dogwood
back of the house, *Don't show all the bones.*

> My brother died, a brown leaf
> against a wire fence.
> My father never got to say goodbye.
> The boy who gave his mouth to me
> saw death in the rear-view mirror,
> turned around to meet it, met it.

Because I daydreamed about how beautiful I'd be
with tears in my eyes.
Because I didn't throw myself over a grenade.
Because of my stupid fault.
How many more have I watched,
helpless, as they were pulled over the falls?

I might have saved them,
might have torn off my senior prom gown
and dived into the torrent.
In front of my horrified eyes
they went over without a sound

80

like a herd of stampeding cattle
crazy with thirst.
Bloody boys, broken women,
thin children,
I might have saved them.

As dawn colors the sky
with sad gray radiance
I count the day I ran to tell Mama
we broke Jamie Crowl's arm on the seesaw,
the day I ran to tell Mama I made Jennifer
take the dangerous shortcut from school,
the day I ran to tell Mama my voodoo had worked.

I remember how she fed me Cheerios
while the news announced in a cold white voice
the numbers of the dead.
How she watched me pore over photographs
of mountains of eyeglasses, mountains of shoes,
then sent me out to play
in the twilight under the streetlamps;
how Junebugs fell heavy and horrible
under by flying feet.

I hear my baby waking up,
trying out my new name like a chant.
Before I face his wonderful eyes
I slip into my raggedy robe
and wash my hands and face.
In the mirror I look like Mama.
I lean closer and look into her eyes:
In their black pupils, I see my grandmother,
her mother, diminishing generations
of the dead, all of them Mama.

I, too, have given my child
to the murderous world.
I go to him, pick him up,
feel in my chest like warm liquid
hundreds of generations of Mama's forgiveness.

OAHE

In Sioux
something firm to stand upon
earthen dams   human
or those in the mind —
so much held back.

How many years did it take
to have it feel good
to be home?
No apologies
I drown
in the warmth
it seeps under my skin
sustains
not quite
till next time.

Oahe Dam
something firm to stand upon
Yet
it holds back
acres and acres   water
that weighs down bones
of sea creatures
buffalo   wolves
pioneers
a bleached mosaic tale
from before the days of salt.

But
what dam living
can hold back sorrow —
acres and acres of tears
or   stem the flood   of error?

Oahe
in Sioux
something firm to stand upon —

For Polly & Wilson
thanks for
love & support
Karen, 1985

WHEN WE WERE SMALL MEDUSAS

Eve, unhappy in the knowledge that she was
  alone in Eden with Adam,
    spoke with snakes.
Emily Dickinson rates snakes Zero
  to the bone and affords to them
    no small cordiality.
And to this day most small girls, women too,
  run if a snake so much as flicks
    its red thread tongue.
But when we were small Medusas,
  my sister and I for sport,
    caught snakes by their tails
And with bare hands, whipped them
  round and round our heads
    until with a wrist snap
The small end lay writhing in our palms
  sep-ar-ate, de-
    tached, like grey smoldering firecrackers.
We would watch the tail squirm,
  hoped it would grow another snake, or
    at least shed skin there
Before our eyes; but we never did watch it
  until it wound down, immobile
    as an old marriage.
We abandoned that sport when
  we married and our daughters
    have never learned it.

THE JANES I KNOW

The Janes I know, far from plain,
are so bright that they light up
worlds when they enter smiling.

But the underside of such brilliance
is the potential for suicide.
Separated from its moorings,
flesh is not a pretty sight.

The capacity for love in the Janes I know
cannot be stopped by simple gestures,
like a finger in a dike
when seas rage, or a kiss
that turns princes to frogs.

The underside of their love
makes hate cause enough to marry.
The Janes I know deny their own destinies,
they wear themselves inside out,
unashamed of bleeding.

NO GIFT GOOD ENOUGH

No gift good enough
to mark eighteen
These, the halcyon days...

One week until college
Jane called remembering
we wish for you
an oriole flashing in green maples
a moonstone that cannot wane

You lived too long
in a basement
the spiders wove webs
with your dreams
the dew could not gather on them
nor your tears create rainbows

Rather you should live always
at the tops of houses
better the widow's walks
than never to surface

Better the attic view
and risk falling
or leaping
than the constant squinting
struggle up
flights of stairs out
of basements.

A LOVE POEM FOR THE NUCLEAR AGE:
AFTER THE BOMB

Sometimes when I am alone
and hear the roar of distant planes,
I think, at last they've come.

And you, my darling, gone,
will never look me in the eyes again.

The red flame wind will drop my house
around me, and my skin.
My skeleton
will briefly bring its bony palm
to its horrific mouth
then fall to dust,

a signal only God the mother sees.

And from the radioactive dust
she'll make a clay undreamed of
and cast me new upon the wheel,
then hand me back to you.

WILD POPPIES

I am afraid to love you,
The taste of wild strawberries
Along the road to Carron
Fades.
The wild poppy, blown by the wind,
Leaves only a stem behind.
Rare gentian bloom and fade
While the brief Burren sun
Turns to mist before midday.
Between the karst crevices,
The hart's tongue fern grows.
I have seen it hiding in the cairns.
Rest here on the dolmen,
Where Irish lovers paused
Breathless in their flight.

I find the windblown petals
Pressed in the pages of my winter book,
I cannot recall the names of flowers,
Dry spectres of summer,
Skeletons etched by neglect.
Their dark remains crumble like butterflies.

GREEN POINSETTIAS

Granny sits and chains and chews for hours.
From her hook and string grow startling afghans,
Tablecloths like weighted snowflakes hang
Round her creaking square oak rocker.
Around the porch ceramic donkeys plod
With cactus burdens heavy under sun.
I study the ruffles of crepe myrtle,
Pink and intricate hedges hiding the house,
Watch the neon spoon chase the blinking dish
Across the sky of steaming summer nights,
And kneed oleo, as the yellow stain
Slides sensuously between my fingers.
On the shelves, no books but a ragged Bible
And a hymnal with "The Old Rugged Cross."
Once a salesman stops and sells us
The Hows and Whys of Hiawatha, lights,
And why the rainbow has no end.
On a shelf, a brazen brass boy pees
Unafraid of the Methodist candlestick.
In winter, my clothes nestle the furnace,
Jutting its square body into the room.
Summers I wash my hair in rainwater
Caught in washtubs by green poinsettias,
I curl my toes on pecan shells and limp
From sandspurs lurking in the stubby grass.
Snakes coil beneath the chinaberry tree
And birds pick figs before preserving time.
Sometimes we get packages from the war:
Carved wooden shoes as blue as sky,
Stories about St. Peter and his switches,
An angry swastika armband.
We make a quilt of embroidered patches,
The Sixth Army next to the Third.
Evenings, H.B. Kaltenborn foghorns
Assaults on beaches where men never swim,
And Roosevelt rocks from this fireplace.
A newsreel says the men are coming home,
And she tells me to tune in "One Man's Family,"
And we will be together again.

SPINDRIFT

I grew up among women,
Soft spoken, like the curves of seashells,
Tough, like sea oats,
Wind battered, hurricane walls,
And shining, mother of pearl.

We gathered,
Sea tendrils,
Cast up on bone sand,
Helpless against the thrusting sea.

Survivors,
Beached driftwood,
Nine aunts stood alone,
Feet planted apart
Against the wind and water.

In a conch shell,
I hear my mother singing
"Daddy's gone a-hunting,"
And we rock together
To the rhythm of waves.

Now,
A family of men,
Heavy with guns and sweat
Sit, elbows on table,
Wear snake boots,
Run deer in orange groves,
Keep good bitches.

In the conch shell
I hear her voice,
"Daddy's gone a-hunting."

TOBY HILL

Sometime between grey skies and sun,
After crocus, before apple blossoms,
Yellow trumpets appear
Pierced by red tulips,
Phrased with the perfume of hyacinths.
A robin seeks last year's seeds,
Miniature muscari
Hide in the grass
Under greening honeysuckle.

In June, heavy heads of peonies,
Bowls of goose feathers,
Downy pink and scarlet-streaked snow
Lean over erect, marching iris,
Row on row in military blue.
Under the dogwood tree,
Memories linger, lilies of the valley,
And blue canterbury bells ring
Clear, true sound like triangles.
Arched behind the stone wall,
Spirea snowflakes fall,
Graceful wands of white.

After chrysanthemums
Are pinched twice,
A streak of scarlet alerts the maple.
Oak hastens to assemble gold,
Apples drop, splitting with sweetness,
For deer to steal come morning mist.
Fire creeps over the woods,
Lights each tree with licking flame.

After the sound of dogs,
Beyond shotgun shells,
Quiet falls with leaves.
Shiny bark fingers clutch,
White descends like a hush.

The seasons pass before my eyes.
Crumbling dirt between my fingers,
I plant imaginary bulbs,
Promises of spring,
In a garden of no more.

BALLAD OF INISHMANN

On the pocked shore by the cliffs of Moher,
The Irish sea is rough and familiar,
A lover whose touch is not forgotten
When time and night have passed.

The launch arrives for a funeral,
Shawled figures in red petticoats,
Wild geraniums among the peat trousers,
Leather faces bowed to scarred rock.

I ache for the child-bride mother,
She crossed the waves in a curragh
To a hospital on the mainland,
Now returns with her stillborn child.

She lays the baby in limestone
They beat into dust for a grave.
They say it takes just two years
Before potatoes will grow.

From the hill they call Synge's chair,
Among rocks where the poet once wrote,
I look out to the fierce sea and dream
While they move from church to grave.

HUMMINGBIRD

The hummingbird flies
like uneven breath.
His throat is the rare hue

of the cardinal flower.
See how the asparagus rises
before distributing

its seed, and the scarred
moon barely visible
in the water, wreathed

by reflections of trees.
Let's swim into the cold
where black loons dive,

two by two, and later,
in the high grass, where
there can be no abstinence,

speak to me the way
a leaf does ascending
in a gust. Say again

how the hummingbird returns
to the same wild grove,
the same magnetic blossoms.

NORTHERN LANDSCAPE

Days longer in light signal
the ears: redwinged blackbirds
return to cattails at Circle Pond,
loud raucous claims stir spiders
from their deep-egg sleep
and a woman wakes under a blur
of wings to remember her husband,
twenty years dead, the way
he would stare off toward the thawing
fields in mid-March, hand poised
on the screen door latch, to catch
the meadowlark's first song,
would smile at her, eyes
reflecting the bird-crossed sky.

All around her, the land waits
and a warmer wind billows her skirt
into a brown design of readiness;
the sun lifts the day into being,
a welcome migration of color
and sound, tulips and daffodils
push another quarter inch
above the leaf-covered beds.
On the back porch she listens
to memory and the punctual beating
of her own steady heart.
A certain openness in her stance
implies belief in things unseen:

on a far fencepost, the favored
bird settles — old-timer with two
essential notes: a slurred descending
whistle she will hear all summer.

THE POET, DISCOURAGED, ENVIES MUSICIANS
"The poet is a failed musician...
who has substituted metaphor for metamorphosis."
— Andrei Sinyavsky

want rhythm. want rhythm
to slide forever up and down
the spinal column, over
the finely-tuned neurons

want hard rock, blues, blue-
grass or golden harp strings
any music of the spheres
want performance and loss

cast off with ease through
energy, want audiences
to tap and sway to voice
or instrument, want drum-

beat and saxophone, piano
mandolin and cello, want
an honest absorption before
everyone in the stance

of a trusted medium, want
late nights to play on,
a natural extension of the
body, want melodies spanning

the connected cells, notes
and changes in the gullible
heart, want sap rising,
shadows and pauses and tonal

resonance, want risk
and hot transformation,
want music to be no pretty
substitute, want poetry.

WHAT TO CALL IT

Within its soaring crystals
snow manufactures seashells
of light: tiny dwellings
for the dead. Fir trees burn
through cold sky, roots
extend through limestone
and well-springs where frogs
twitch unconsciously in mud
and you, you crave intimacy
again, wish to stretch infinitely
the space between two points.

Still, you had come to view
that intensity as distraction
which, like illness,
disowns all common purpose.
You had learned to prefer
yourself, requiring nothing.
And now you're only half-
convinced, spent as in
an aftermath from speed
or in a picture swirling
with Van Gogh's blue wind
and yellow stars, startled
and battered by the dense
energy which moves you.
Call it destiny or time;
call it uncertainty if you like.
Call it whatever enters your life.

WEDDING REHEARSAL
(for Allison and Scott)

The minister from the city
arrives first.
The grey stones of the chapel
glow with their usual somberness
but stormclouds have disbanded
leaving only a sketch of turbulence
in the upper sky.

There is no key for entering
here — when the doors
finally open, cooler air
slides through.
Just out of reach,
the nests of the siskins
take root in the branches.

We face southward
awaiting the bride.
She steps up brilliant
in the midst of friends,
a purple sash around
her red silk dress.

The minister smiles knowingly.
"Would you like to practice
the kiss again. . . .?"
astonished always to find
he is marrying two
so like himself.
His voice magnifies
in the silence
before the vows are spoken
as the late afternoon light
begins to absorb the colors
from the oncoming day.

A CUBIST ANALYSIS

The illusion of richness
comes from our compact natures:
roll them out my dear
and you'll see
the cluttered dailiness of our lives together.
Time unfolds the will to dominate,
like an infinite regression of violins,
as well as the occasional
fat pear of nurture
waiting in its porcelain dish
for the edge of a fruit knife.

WHAT SHE GAVE ME

Momma never
never worried about
what other people thought.
We learned early
to sit eyes down,
through arguments with:
      waiters, cashiers, parking
      lot attendants, department
      store managers, teachers
and so on.
Her principles were deep-rooted,
lack of logic in others served only to make her
more relentless in her quest
to provide total enlightenment.
Most of her battles were confined
to questions of taxable items
on grocery receipts
or the fair price of
inferior Christmas trees,
but once, Momma's contentiousness
made her shine.

I was six years old and we
were sightseeing New Orleans
on a hot winter day
but it was green, green
and cool in the heathen cathedral
with novena candles everywhere and
the aboveground graves out back.
Then, bright sun,
and for us two younger ones
on to an amusement park
with pony rides for being so good.
"Hey, honey, want a free turn? Not you
black boy, get out of here."

Momma, as usual unafraid
of confrontation,
grabbed my arm,
but this time
the shrill bluster was gone.
"No she does not,
not if he can't."
We got ice cream instead.

Years later she and I argue about:
      welfare mothers, nuclear
      disarmament, childrearing,
      sex, religion, Central America.
and so on.
But it's her fault,
and her starry crown.

MOTHERSONG

Child, I don't know you yet
nor even love you.
Stranger shuttling in my belly,
you weave through my thoughts,
change my body's shape,
send me to that underground place
where pregnant women live
and move like weighted dreams.
I break favorite cups,
can't write a decent line,
have spider veins on my legs;
all these signs point
to the birth of one
in whom my moon and stars will reside:
an ordinary child.

FALL BREW

When the fall wind arrives
flamboyant but threadbare,
like an aging actor
on a smalltown tour, and
my house's frame
stiffens and knots,
I take marrow bones
braise them in fat,
make rich brown broth
and sprinkle the house with its
oily steam.
Muttering protective incantations
of my own devising,
I reach for and miss
the charred wisdom of my mothers.
Still, my babies sleep
warm and sound at night,
the dog's coat gleams,
the house breathes slowly,
the mothers are smiling.

THREE TIMES I UNDERSTOOD DEATH

I.

There was
a small, still animal
matted fur
lips pulled back
teeth white
and curved
desiccated
in the quiet
desert heat.

II.

There were
neon leaves
greywash clouds
a slick black road
moving
to a sudden horizon.

III.

The bird
and the dead tree
were black
against
a solid blue sky.
The bird sang
two notes.
A Japanese woman
and I
walked backward
to watch.

MARY EASTER divides her professional life between teaching dance at Carleton College, Northfield, Minnesota, and performing as an independent artist. She has toured widely in her solo concert MARY EASTER DANCES. Her current choreographic work combines movement with her own writings.

ANDREA EEN is a professional violinist and a violist, conductor, and teacher at St. Olaf College, Northfield, Minnesota, who has a special interest in the traditional music of the Norwegian Hardanger Fiddle and has studied with fiddlers in Norway. She has been writing poetry for the past five years.

THEONA GERY brought to her poetry her love of children, of beauty, and her closeness to nature. After illness shut down the teaching career she loved, she began to write poetry. Tee's death in 1981 left a legacy of memories of her quiet strength as well as a body of strong poetry.

BONNIE KELTERBORN views her main role in life as that of a teacher. Trained in mathematics, she has taught many different courses — education, psychology, the future. She brings her deeply held beliefs about justice into all these fields. Currently she is doing medical research as a post-doctoral "fellow" in Biometry and she is writing a book, a pioneering effort in psychology.

NORA KERR was raised "all over the eastern seaboard and Mexico." She wrote her first poem in Spanish at age eight, a declaration of love to her nursemaid. She continued to write sporadically, mostly about love and/or misery, while getting a BS and MS in linguistics from Georgetown University, adopting and raising a daughter, and working as a faculty member/administrator at various colleges. She began to write regularly and seriously in 1980.

SIGI LEONHARD was born in Germany and pursued her education there, in France, and at Stanford University. She teaches German at Carleton College in Northfield, Minnesota. While always interested in writing poetry and short prose, scholarly writing has demanded most of her time until recently. Now she is trying to achieve a balance between scholarly and creative writing.

RIKI KOLBL NELSON is a poet and visual artist (batik, watercolor, sculpture), who has been writing since age sixteen as a way to keep in touch with her inner life. She has recently begun to write bi-lingual dialect poems to conquer her nostalgia for Austria where she grew up. She has published poems, exhibited her art work, conducted writing workshops, and co-edited a poetry magazine.

SUSAN MARIE SWANSON became a member of Northfield Women Poets when she was a student at St. Olaf College in the mid-seventies. Now she lives in St. Paul where she cares for her young son, leads a weekly poetry meeting for a group of mentally retarded women, and occasionally ventures out on poetry residencies for COMPAS Writers in the Schools. She has received a Loft McKnight Award and a Bush Foundation Fellowship.

106

MARCELLA TAYLOR teaches creative writing, modern literature, and film studies at St. Olaf College in Northfield. Her volume of poetry, *The Lost Daughter,* will be published in the fall of 1984 by the Renaissance Press in Chicago. She presently lives with a nephew and a cat in an old house on the Cannon River in Northfield. The poems included in this anthology were written during a Fulbright year in Europe.

M. VOGL GERY is a former Mentor winner at The Loft in Minneapolis and the recipient of a Minnesota State Arts Board grant. She currently is working on the final stories in her book *The Woman Tree.* Writer, wife, mother, and teacher, Marie has published several poems and stories over the past twelve years.

BEVERLY VOLDSETH was born in 1935 of immigrant parents. The fifth of seven children, the first to graduate from high school, the only one to attend college, she arranges words on paper to exorcize the ghosts of the past and record the present. She edits the *Rag Mag.*

MARILYN WANIEK taught English at St. Olaf College from 1973 to 1978, and is now in the English department at the University of Connecticut. Her first book of poems, *For the Body,* was published by LSU Press in 1978. She is a co-translator of Danish childrens' stories, the recipient of an NEA Creative Writing Fellowship and a poetry residency at Yaddo, and the mother of a young son.

KAREN HERSETH WEE was born and grew up in rural South Dakota, eldest child of three. Nurtured to be a farmer, she got waylaid by a college education and has been associated somehow with St. Olaf College in Northfield almost ever since. Co-creator of Northfield Women Poets, her poems began to come about the same time that her three children did, and because of them.

NENA THAMES WHITTEMORE grew up as an "army brat" and has lived in Japan as well as in many parts of the United States. After graduating from Carleton College in 1961, she moved east. Returning to Carleton in 1976, she became the Director of Alumni Affairs. She vacillates between poetry and fundraising and is presently the Executive Director of Development and College Relations at Hollins College, Roanoke, Virginia.

JOAN WOLF graduated from Carleton College in 1971 and received an MFA from Goddard College in 1977. She has been a teacher for several years and currently teaches at a psychiatric hospital for adolescents. She is a former Mentor poet winner at the Loft in Minneapolis. Her book of poems, *The Divided Sphere,* is from Floating Island Press. She has one son, Shawn.

TRINA ZELLE constantly works at integrating into a coherent whole the roles of wife, mother, poet, ordained Presbyterian minister and wild woman. She draws comfort from the knowledge that it is her commonality with other women that is the source of her best work.